Chenrezig
SADHANA & COMMENTARY

The Practice Text
*Extending Throughout Space
for the Benefit of Beings*
by Tangtong Gyalpo

The Commentary
Continual Rain for the Benefit of Beings
by Khakhyab Dorjé, the 15th Karmapa

Translated under the guidance of
Shamar Rinpoché
by Pamela Gayle White

Second edition (hardcover)
Bird of Paradise Press
Lexington, Virginia

Chenrezig Sadhana and Commentary

Second Edition (Hardcover) Copyright © Bird of Paradise Press, 2020

Original Edition Copyright © Bodhi Path Buddhist Centers, 2012

Natural Bridge, Virginia, USA

ISBN: 978-1-7347823-4-9

Bird of Paradise Press, 1223 N. Lee Highway, #250, Lexington, Virginia, 24450 USA

www.birdofparadisepress.org

Translated from Tibetan by Pamela Gayle White under the guidance of Shamar Rinpoche. Tibetan phonetics by Pamela Gayle White.

Edited by the Thöding Translation Group

Original Tibetan texts:

Sadhana: *Extending Throughout Space for the Benefit of Beings* (*'Gro don mkha' khyab ma*) by Tangtong Gyalpo (Thang stong rgyal po)

Commentary: *Continual Rain for the Benefit of Beings* (*'Gro don char rgyun*) by the 15th Karmapa, Khakhyab Dorjé (mKha' khyab rdo rje)

Cover and book design by Carol Gerhardt

Adapted for hardcover by Annie Heckman

Chenrezig

OM   MA   NI   PAD   ME   HUNG

Introduction

As one of the Buddha Shakyamuni's eight close disciples, Chenrezig—Avalokiteshvara in Sanskrit—was present when the Buddha gave teachings on the Bodhisattvayana.

Chenrezig is a tenth bhumi bodhisattva: one whose realization is so luminous and complete that he is endowed with all of the qualities of a Buddha and could be considered fully enlightened. His vow is to remain in samsara until all beings have been freed from the agony and confusion of cyclic existence. Because he manifests as a perfectly realized bodhisattva, his activity is to use every possible means to lead beings to liberation in whichever form is most expedient. When the Buddha was on Vulture Peak in Rajgir giving the teachings on Prajnaparamita—transcendent knowledge—Avalokita was there in the form of a human monk; where tantric Buddhist methods have been most useful, he has manifested as a yidam, or meditation deity.

His many forms—two, four or a thousand arms; white, red and so on—correspond with the varying needs and predispositions of practitioners. Whichever of his practices is chosen, we have his promise that if we endeavor to follow his example, all gates to rebirth in the three unfortunate realms will be definitively shut and sooner or later we will reach enlightenment.

The meditation-recitation of four-armed Chenrezig given here is a particularly effective practice method for human beings. Its lineage originates with the 15th-century Tibetan mahasiddha Tangtong Gyalpo, who was Chenrezig himself in human form. It belongs to the 'gom-loung' class, meaning that we may engage in the practice without having first received an empowerment. Though it is quite accessible and easy to follow, this concise form of the Chenrezig meditation-recitation can ultimately lead to the same deep realization and results as far more elaborate Chenrezig practices.

The 15th Gyalwa Karmapa, Khakhyab Dorjé (1871–1922) was an emanation of Chenrezig. One of many stories that illustrate his connection with the deity speaks of a site consecration connected with Pongphuk monastery in Létang, eastern Tibet, near Yunnan. The Karmapa, who was far away in his monastery in Tshurphu, central Tibet, had been invited to bless the land where new buildings were to be built. Although he could not travel to Pongphuk, he sent the message that the people there should prepare everything as if Chenrezig himself was coming to perform the blessing ritual. And so it was: from the tormas to the music to the welcoming committee, everything was done according to tradition.

When the time came for the part of the blessing where the master of ceremonies throws consecrated rice on the ground which is to be blessed, Karmapa Khakhyab Dorjé, inseparable from Chenrezig, threw the rice in Tsurphu . . . and it landed in Pongphuk. The rice was immediately gathered by the people attending the ceremony and carefully stored as an extraordinarily great blessing. It was considered so holy that although people were offered great sums of money for it, no one would part with their miraculous rice. The incident was seen as additional proof that the 15th Karmapa was none other than Chenrezig himself.

Khakhyab Dorjé wrote the commentary presented in this book with the wish that whoever practices the Chenrezig meditation will reach Chenrezig's pure realm, Potala Mountain, with no hindrances or obstacles.

With all of this in mind, I have taken the initiative to translate the Chenrezig practice and commentary into English with the help of Pamela Gayle White.

—Shamar Rinpoché

The Mahasiddha Tangtong Gyalpo

ༀༀ། ཕྱགས་རྗེ་ཆེན་པོའི་བསྒོམ་བཟླས་
འགྲོ་དོན་མཁའ་ཁྱབ་མ་བཞུགས་སོ །།

སངས་རྒྱས་ཆོས་དང་ཚོགས་ཀྱི་མཆོག་རྣམས་ལ།།

sangyé chötang tsok kyi chok nam la

བྱང་ཆུབ་བར་དུ་བདག་ནི་སྐྱབས་སུ་མཆི།།

jangchoub bardou dani kyab sou chi

བདག་གིས་སྦྱིན་སོགས་བགྱིས་པའི་བསོད་ནམས་ཀྱི།།

dagi jinso gyipé sönam kyi

འགྲོ་ལ་ཕན་ཕྱིར་སངས་རྒྱས་འགྲུབ་པར་ཤོག།

drola penchir sangyé droubpar sho

Chenrezig Sadhana

Extending Throughout Space for the Benefit of Beings:
the Meditation-Recitation of Great Compassion

We begin the Chenrezig meditation-recitation by taking refuge and developing bodhicitta.

Repeat three times.

Until I have reached full awakening, I take refuge
in the Buddha, the Dharma and the supreme Assembly.
Through the merit resulting from such practices
as generosity,
may I attain enlightenment in order to benefit beings.

བདག་སོགས་མཁའ་ཁྱབ་སེམས་ཅན་གྱི།

daso khakhyab semchen gyi

སྤྱི་གཙུག་པད་དཀར་ཟླ་བའི་སྟེང་།

chitsouk pékar dawé téng

ཧྲཱིཿལས་འཕགས་མཆོག་སྤྱན་རས་གཟིགས།

hri lé pak chok chenrézik

དཀར་གསལ་འོད་ཟེར་ལྔ་ལྡན་འཕྲོ།

karsel öser nga den tro

མཛེས་འཛུམ་ཐུགས་རྗེའི་སྤྱན་གྱིས་གཟིགས།

dzé dzoum touk jé'i chen gyi zik

ཕྱག་བཞིའི་དང་པོ་ཐལ་སྦྱར་མཛེད།

chak shi'i dangpo taljar dzé

འོག་གཉིས་ཤེལ་ཕྲེང་པད་དཀར་རྣམས།

ok nyi sheltréng pékar nam

དར་དང་རིན་ཆེན་རྒྱན་གྱིས་སྤྲས།

dar tang rinchen gyen gyi tré

རི་དགས་ལྤགས་པའི་སྟོད་གཡོགས་གསོལ།

ridak pakpé tö yo söl

འོད་དཔག་མེད་པའི་དབུ་རྒྱན་ཅན།

öpa mépé ougyen chen

ཞབས་གཉིས་རྡོ་རྗེའི་སྐྱིལ་ཀྲུང་བཞུགས།

shiab nyi dordjé'i kyil troung zhouk

དྲི་མེད་ཟླ་བར་རྒྱབ་བརྟེན་པ།

drimé dawar gyab tenpa

སྐྱབས་གནས་ཀུན་འདུས་ངོ་བོར་གྱུར།

kyab né kün dü ngowor gyour

We create
the deity
visualization.

Upon a white lotus and moon above my head
and crowning each sentient being throughout space,
is HRI from which Noble, Supreme Chenrezig appears,
gleaming white and radiating five-colored light.
Lovely and smiling, he gazes with eyes of compassion.
The first two of his four hands are held palms together,
the lower two hold a crystal rosary and white lotus.
Adorned with silk and jewel ornaments,
his upper body is clothed with a deerskin.
His head is crowned with Buddha Amitabha,
and he is seated in the adamantine posture
with an immaculate full moon as his backrest.
In essence he is the union of all sources of refuge.

བདག་དང་སེམས་ཅན
ཐམས་ཅད་ཀྱིས་མགྲིན
གཅིག་ཏུ་གསོལ་བ་
འདེབས་པར་བསམས
ཁ།།

ཞེས་ཅི་ནུས་བཟླག་ག།

ཛོ་བོ་སྐྱོན་གྱིས་མ་གོས་སྐུ་མདོག་དཀར།
jowo kyön gyi magö koundok kar

རྫོགས་སངས་རྒྱས་ཀྱི་དབུ་ལ་བརྒྱན།
dzok sangyé kyi oula gyen

ཐུགས་རྗེའི་སྤྱན་གྱིས་འགྲོ་ལ་བཟིགས།
toukjé'i chen gyi dro la zik

སྤྱན་རས་གཟིགས་ལ་ཕྱག་འཚལ་ལོ།།
chenrézik la chak tsello

འཕགས་པ་སྤྱན་རས་གཟིགས་དབང་དང་།།
pakpa chenrézik wang tang

ཕྱོགས་བཅུ་དུས་གསུམ་བཞུགས་པ་ཡི།།
chok chou düsoum zhoukpa yi

རྒྱལ་བ་སྲས་བཅས་ཐམས་ཅད་ལ།།
gyalwa séché tamché la

ཀུན་ནས་དང་བས་ཕྱག་འཚལ་ལོ།།
künné dangwé chak tsallo

མེ་ཏོག་བདུག་སྤོས་མར་མེ་དྲི།།
métok doukpö marmé dri

ཞལ་ཟས་རོལ་མོ་ལ་སོགས་པ།།
zhalzé rölmo la sok pa

དངོས་འབྱོར་ཡིད་ཀྱིས་སྤྲུལ་ནས་འབུལ།།
ngö djor yikyi trül né bül

འཕགས་པའི་ཚོགས་ཀྱིས་བཞེས་སུ་གསོལ།།
pakpé tsok kyi zhé sou söl

We imagine that
we are praying in
unison with all
sentient beings:

*We recite this as
much as we can.*

Lord of pure white, undefiled and flawless,
your head is crowned with the perfect Buddha.
You gaze upon beings with eyes of compassion:
Chenrezig, I bow down before you.

The seven
branch prayer:

With perfect sincerity, I bow down
before the Noble Lord Chenrezig
and all of the Buddhas and Bodhisattvas
of the three times and ten directions.

Noble Assembly, please accept these gifts
of flowers, incense, butter lamps, fragrance,
fine foods, music and the like, along with
all of the offerings called forth by my mind.

ཐོག་མ་མེད་ནས་ད་ལྟའི་བར།

tokma méné daté bar

མི་དགེ་བཅུ་དང་མཚམས་མེད་ལྔ།

migé chou tang tsammé nga

སེམས་ནི་ཉོན་མོངས་དབང་གྱུར་པའི།

semni nyönmong wang gyour pé

སྡིག་པ་ཐམས་ཅད་བཤགས་པར་བགྱི།

dikpa tamché shakpar gyi

ཉན་ཐོས་རང་རྒྱལ་བྱང་ཆུབ་སེམས།

nyen tö rang gyal jangchoub sem

སོ་སོ་སྐྱེ་བོ་ལ་སོགས་པས།

soso kyéwo la sok pé

དུས་གསུམ་དགེ་བ་ཅི་བསགས་པའི།

düsoum géwa chi sak pé

བསོད་ནམས་ལ་ནི་བདག་ཡི་རང་།

sönam lani dayi rang

སེམས་ཅན་རྣམས་ཀྱི་བསམ་པ་དང་།

semchen namkyi sampa tang

བློ་ཡི་བྱེ་བྲག་ཇི་ལྟ་བར།

loyi jédrak ji ta war

ཆེ་ཆུང་ཐུན་མོང་ཐེག་པ་ཡི།

chéchoung tünmong tékpa yi

ཆོས་ཀྱི་འཁོར་ལོ་བསྐོར་དུ་གསོལ།

chökyi khorlo kor tou söl

འཁོར་བ་ཇི་སྲིད་མ་སྟོངས་བར།

khorwa jisi ma tong war

མྱ་ངན་མི་འདའ་ཐུགས་རྗེ་ཡིས།

nya ngen mi da touk jé yi

སྡུག་བསྔལ་རྒྱ་མཚོར་བྱིང་བ་ཡི།

douk ngal gyatsor jing wa yi

སེམས་ཅན་རྣམས་ལ་བཟིགས་སུ་གསོལ།

semchen nam la zik sou söl

I disclose each and every misdeed I've committed
under the influence of disturbing emotions—
the ten non-virtuous acts and five boundless offenses—
from beginningless time till the present.

I rejoice in all merit accumulated
through the past, present and future good conduct
of Shravakas, Pratyekabuddhas, Bodhisattvas,
ordinary people and all other beings.

Please turn the wheel of the Dharma
of the greater, lesser and common vehicles
in keeping with the different motivations
and aptitudes of sentient beings.

Please do not pass into Nirvana
until Samsara has been emptied.
Kindly watch over all beings
who are engulfed in the ocean of suffering.

བདག་གིས་བསོད་ནམས་ཅི་བསགས་པ།།

dagi sönam chi sak pa

ཐམས་ཅད་བྱང་ཆུབ་རྒྱུར་གྱུར་ནས།།

tamché jangchoub gyour gyour né

རིང་པོར་མི་ཐོགས་འགྲོ་བ་ཡི།།

ring por mitok drowa yi

འདྲེན་པའི་དཔལ་དུ་བདག་གྱུར་ཅིག།

drenpé pal dou dagyour chik

དགེ་སློང་པ་ཀུ་དཀར་ པོའི་ཕྱག་ནས་དགུན་ རས་གཟིགས་ཀྱི་གསོལ་ འདེབས་སོ།།

གསོལ་བ་འདེབས་སོ་བླ་མ་སྤྱན་རས་གཟིགས།།

sölwa deb so lama chenrézik

གསོལ་བ་འདེབས་སོ་ཡི་དམ་སྤྱན་རས་གཟིགས།།

sölwa deb so yidam chenrézik

གསོལ་བ་འདེབས་སོ་འཕགས་མཆོག་སྤྱན་རས་གཟིགས།།

sölwa deb so pak chok chenrézik

གསོལ་བ་འདེབས་སོ་སྐྱབས་མཆོག་སྤྱན་རས་གཟིགས།།

sölwa deb so kyab chok chenrézik

གསོལ་བ་འདེབས་སོ་བྱམས་མགོན་སྤྱན་རས་གཟིགས།།

sölwa deb so jam gön chenrézik

ཐུགས་རྗེ་བཟུང་ཤིག་རྒྱལ་བ་ཐུགས་རྗེ་ཅན།།

touk jé zoung shik gyalwa touk jé chen

མཐའ་མེད་འཁོར་བར་གྲངས་མེད་འཁྱམས་གྱུར་ཅིང་།།

tamé khorwar drang mé khyam gyour ching

བཟོད་མེད་སྡུག་བསྔལ་མྱོང་བའི་འགྲོ་བ་ལ།།

zömé douk ngal nyong wé drowa la

མགོན་པོ་ཁྱེད་ལས་སྐྱབས་གཞན་མ་མཆིས་སོ།།

gönpo khyé lé kyab zhen ma chi so

རྣམ་མཁྱེན་སངས་རྒྱས་ཐོབ་པར་བྱིན་གྱིས་རློབས།།

nam khyen sangyé tobpar jingyi lob

16

May whatever merit I have gathered
be the cause for universal awakening.
May I become an outstanding guide for beings
without any further delay.

Gélong Péma
Karpo's prayer to
his practice deity
Chenrezig:

I pray to you, Lama Chenrezig,
I pray to you, Yidam Chenrezig,
I pray to you, Noble, Supreme Chenrezig,
I pray to you, Supreme Refuge Chenrezig,
I pray to you, Loving Protector Chenrezig:
kindly look after us, Victorious Compassionate One.

O Protector, we who have wandered
countless times through endless samsara
and experienced its unbearable suffering
have no other refuge than you.
Please bless us so that we may attain
the omniscience of the enlightened state.

ཐོག་མེད་དུས་ནས་ལས་ངན་བསགས་པའི་མཐུས།།

tok mé dü né lé ngen sakpé tü

ཞེ་སྡང་དབང་གིས་དམྱལ་བར་སྐྱེས་གྱུར་ཏེ།

zhédang wang gi nyalwar kyé gyour té

ཚ་གྲང་སྡུག་བསྔལ་མྱོང་བའི་སེམས་ཅན་རྣམས།།

tsadrang douk ngal nyong wé semchen nam

ལྷ་མཆོག་ཁྱེད་ཀྱི་དྲུང་དུ་སྐྱེ་བར་ཤོག།

lha chok khyé kyi droung dou kyéwar sho

ཨོཾ་མ་ཎི་པདྨེ་ཧཱུྃ།

om mani padmé houng

ཐོག་མེད་དུས་ནས་ལས་ངན་བསགས་པའི་མཐུས།།

tok mé dü né lé ngen sakpé tü

སེར་སྣའི་དབང་གིས་ཡི་དྭགས་གནས་སུ་སྐྱེ།

serné wang gi yidak né sou kyé

བཀྲེས་སྐོམ་སྡུག་བསྔལ་མྱོང་བའི་སེམས་ཅན་རྣམས།།

trékom douk ngal nyong wé semchen nam

ཞིང་མཆོག་པོ་ཏ་ལ་རུ་སྐྱེ་བར་ཤོག།

zhing chok potala rou kyéwar sho

ཨོཾ་མ་ཎི་པདྨེ་ཧཱུྃ།

om mani padmé houng

ཐོག་མེད་དུས་ནས་ལས་ངན་བསགས་པའི་མཐུས།།

tok mé dü né lé ngen sakpé tü

གཏི་མུག་དབང་གིས་དུད་འགྲོར་སྐྱེས་གྱུར་ཏེ།

timouk wang gi düdror kyé gyour té

ལེན་ཀོག་སྡུག་བསྔལ་མྱོང་བའི་སེམས་ཅན་རྣམས།།

len kouk douk ngal nyongwé semchen nam

མགོན་པོ་ཁྱེད་ཀྱི་དྲུང་དུ་སྐྱེ་བར་ཤོག།

gönpo khyé kyi droung dou kyéwar sho

ཨོཾ་མ་ཎི་པདྨེ་ཧཱུྃ།

om mani padmé houng

Due to negative karma collected throughout
beginningless time,
anger and aggression have resulted in rebirth
in the hell realms.
May those beings who experience the torment
of great heat and cold
be reborn in your presence, Supreme Deity.
Om Mani Padmé Hung.

Due to negative karma collected throughout
beginningless time,
miserliness has resulted in rebirth
in the hungry ghost realms.
May those beings who experience the torment
of hunger and thirst
be reborn in the supreme realm of Potala.
Om Mani Padmé Hung.

Due to negative karma collected throughout
beginningless time,
extreme dullness has resulted in rebirth
among the animals.
May those beings who experience the torment
of being speechless and dull
be reborn in your presence, O Protector.
Om Mani Padmé Hung.

ཐོག་མེད་དུས་ནས་ལས་ངན་བསགས་པའི་མཐུས།།

tok mé dü né lé ngen sakpé tü

འདོད་ཆགས་དབང་གིས་མི་ཡི་གནས་སུ་སྐྱེ།།

döchak wang gi miyi né sou kyé

བྲེལ་ཕོངས་སྡུག་བསྔལ་མྱོང་བའི་སེམས་ཅན་རྣམས།།

drelpong douk ngal nyong wé semchen nam

ཞིང་མཆོག་བདེ་བ་ཅན་དུ་སྐྱེ་བར་ཤོག།

zhing chok déwachen dou kyéwar sho

ༀ་མ་ཎི་པདྨེ་ཧཱུྃ།

om mani padmé houng

ཐོག་མེད་དུས་ནས་ལས་ངན་བསགས་པའི་མཐུས།།

tok mé dü né lé ngen sakpé tü

ཕྲག་དོག་དབང་གིས་ལྷ་མིན་གནས་སུ་སྐྱེ།།

tradok wang gi lhamin né sou kyé

འཐབ་རྩོད་སྡུག་བསྔལ་མྱོང་བའི་སེམས་ཅན་རྣམས།།

tab tsö douk ngal nyong wé semchen nam

པོ་ཏ་ལ་ཡི་ཞིང་དུ་སྐྱེ་བར་ཤོག།

potala yi zhing dou kyéwar sho

ༀ་མ་ཎི་པདྨེ་ཧཱུྃ།

om mani padmé houng

ཐོག་མེད་དུས་ནས་ལས་ངན་བསགས་པའི་མཐུས།།

tok mé dü né lé ngen sakpé tü

ང་རྒྱལ་དབང་གིས་ལྷ་ཡི་གནས་སུ་སྐྱེ།།

ngagyal wang gi lha yi né sou kyé

འགྲོ་ལྡུང་སྡུག་བསྔལ་མྱོང་བའི་སེམས་ཅན་རྣམས།།

potoung douk ngal nyong wé semchen nam

པོ་ཏ་ལ་ཡི་ཞིང་དུ་སྐྱེ་བར་ཤོག།

potala yi zhing dou kyéwar sho

ༀ་མ་ཎི་པདྨེ་ཧཱུྃ།

om mani padmé houng

Due to negative karma collected throughout
beginningless time,
desire and attachment have resulted in rebirth
in the human world.
May those beings who experience the anguish
of poverty and toil
be reborn in Dewachen, the supreme realm of bliss.
Om Mani Padmé Hung.

Due to negative karma collected throughout
beginningless time,
intense envy has resulted in rebirth
in the realms of the demi-gods.
May those beings who experience the anguish
of rivalry and quarrels
be reborn in the pure realm of Potala.
Om Mani Padmé Hung.

Due to negative karma collected throughout
beginningless time,
great pride has resulted in rebirth among the god realms.
May those beings who experience the anguish
of transition and descent
be reborn in the pure realm of Potala.
Om Mani Padmé Hung.

བདག་ནི་སྐྱེ་ཞིང་སྐྱེ་བ་ཐམས་ཅད་དུ།།

dani kyé shing kyéwa tamché dou

སྤྱན་རས་གཟིགས་དང་མཛད་པ་མཚུངས་པ་ཡིས།།

chenrézik tang dzépa tsoungpa yi

མ་དག་ཞིང་གི་འགྲོ་རྣམས་སྒྲོལ་བ་དང་།།

madak zhing gi dronam drölwa tang

གསུང་མཆོག་ཡིག་དྲུག་ཕྱོགས་བཅུར་རྒྱས་བྱེད་ཤོག།

soung chok yik drouk chok chour gyé jé sho

འཕགས་མཆོག་ཁྱེད་ལ་གསོལ་བ་བཏབ་པའི་མཐུས།།

pak chok khyé la sölwa tabpé tü

བདག་གི་གདུལ་བྱར་གྱུར་པའི་འགྲོ་བ་རྣམས།།

dagi düljar gyourpé drowa nam

ལས་འབྲས་ལྷུར་ལེན་དགེ་བའི་ལས་ལ་བརྩོན།།

léndré lhour len géwé lé la tsön

འགྲོ་བའི་དོན་དུ་ཆོས་དང་ལྡན་པར་ཤོག།

drowé döndou chötang denpar sho

As I continue along from one life to the next,
may I liberate the beings of the impure realms
by virtue of activity similar to Chenrezig's,
and may I fill the whole of the ten directions
with the supreme speech of the six syllables.

By the power of my prayers to you, Great Noble One,
may those who are destined to be trained by me
carefully observe the law of cause and effect
and always strive to accomplish goodness.
May they uphold the Dharma for the benefit of beings.

དེ་ལྟར་རྩེ་གཅིག་གསོལ་བཏབ་པས།།

détar tséchik söl tab pé

འཕགས་པའི་སྐུ་ལས་འོད་ཟེར་འཕྲོས།།

pakpé koulé özer trö

མ་དག་ལས་ནང་འཁྲུལ་ཤེས་སྦྱང་།།

madak lénang trül shé jang

ཕྱི་སྣོད་བདེ་བ་ཅན་གྱི་ཞིང་།།

chinö déwachen gyi zhing

ནང་བཅུད་སྐྱེ་འགྲོའི་ལུས་ངག་སེམས།།

nang chü kyé dro'i lü ngak sem

སྤྱན་རས་གཟིགས་དབང་སྐུ་གསུང་ཐུགས།།

chenrézik wang kou soung touk

སྣང་གྲགས་རིག་སྟོང་དབྱེར་མེད་གྱུར།།

nang drak rik tong yermé gyour

ཨོཾ་མ་ཎི་པདྨེ་ཧཱུྃ

OM MANI PADMÉ HOUNG

བདག་གཞན་ལུས་སྣང་འཕགས་པའི་སྐུ།།

dazhen lünang pakpé kou

སྒྲ་གྲགས་ཡི་གེ་དྲུག་པའི་དབྱངས།།

dradrak yigé droukpé yang

དྲན་རྟོག་ཡེ་ཤེས་ཆེན་པོའི་ཀློང་།།

drentok yéshé chenpo'i long

དགེ་བ་འདི་ཡིས་མྱུར་དུ་བདག།

géwa diyi nyourdou da

སྤྱན་རས་གཟིགས་དབང་འགྲུབ་གྱུར་ནས།།

chenrézik wang droup gyour né

འགྲོ་བ་གཅིག་ཀྱང་མ་ལུས་པ།།

drowa chik kyang malüpa

དེ་ཡི་ས་ལ་འགོད་པར་ཤོག།

déyi sala göpar sho

As the result of this perfectly focused invocation,
light radiates from the body of the Noble One
clearing away impure karmic experience
and misconceptions.
The outer universe manifests as Dewachen,
the Realm of Joy,
and the body, speech and mind of the beings
who live there
are the enlightened body, speech and mind
of Lord Chenrezig.
Appearance, sound and awareness are
inseparable from emptiness.

OM MANI PADMÉ HUNG

We meditate
on the meaning
of this while
reciting as many
Om Mani Padmé
Hung mantras
as possible.

Our physical forms are the body of the Noble One,
all sounds are the melody of the six syllables,
and thoughts are the vast expanse of great wisdom.

Through this virtue, may I swiftly attain
the state of Lord Chenrezig,
and may I establish all beings,
without a single exception, in this state.

Finally, we settle
in the meditative
equanimity of
the essential state,
with no concept
of subject, object,
or action.

ཨེ་མ་ཧོ༔

é ma ho

ངོ་མཚར་སངས་རྒྱས་སྣང་བ་མཐའ་ཡས་དང་།

ngotsar sangyé nangwa tayé tang

གཡས་སུ་ཇོ་བོ་ཐུགས་རྗེ་ཆེན་པོ་དང་།

yésou jowo toukjé chenpo tang

གཡོན་དུ་སེམས་དཔའ་མཐུ་ཆེན་ཐོབ་རྣམས་ལ།

yöndou sempa touchen tob nam la

སངས་རྒྱས་བྱང་སེམས་དཔག་མེད་འཁོར་གྱིས་བསྐོར།

sangyé jangsem pakmé khor gyi kor

བདེ་སྐྱིད་ངོ་མཚར་དཔག་ཏུ་མེད་པ་ཡི།

dékyi ngotsar paktou mépa yi

བདེ་བ་ཅན་ཞེས་བྱ་བའི་ཞིང་ཁམས་དེར།

déwachen zhé jawé zhing kham dér

བདག་ནི་འདི་ནས་ཚེ་འཕོས་གྱུར་མ་ཐག

dani diné tsé pö gyour ma tak

སྐྱེ་བ་གཞན་གྱིས་བར་མ་ཆོད་པ་རུ།

kyéwa zhen gyi barma chö pa rou

དེ་རུ་སྐྱེས་ནས་སྣང་མཐའི་ཞལ་མཐོང་ཤོག

dérou kyéné nang té zheltong sho

དེ་སྐད་བདག་གིས་སྨོན་ལམ་བཏབ་པ་འདི།

déké dagi mönlam tabpa di

ཕྱོགས་བཅུའི་སངས་རྒྱས་བྱང་སེམས་ཐམས་ཅད་ཀྱིས།

chok chou'i sangyé jangsem tamché kyi

གེགས་མེད་འགྲུབ་པར་བྱིན་གྱིས་བརླབ་ཏུ་གསོལ།

gékmé droubpar jingyi lab tou söl

ཏདྱཐཱ༔ པཉྩནྡྲི་ཡ་ཨ་ཝ་བོ་དྷ་ན་ཡེ་སྭཱ་ཧཱ།

tayata pentsadriya awa bodhanayé soha

É Ma Ho!
Amazing! Amitabha, the Buddha of Infinite Light,
with Chenrezig, the Great Compassionate Lord,
to his right
and Vajrapani, the Bodhisattva of Great Powers,
to his left,
all surrounded by innumerable Buddhas and
Bodhisattvas!

As soon as I have left this existence behind,
without the interval of another life, may I take birth
in that wondrous Pure Land, the Realm of Joy,
the place of everlasting happiness called Dewachen,
and may I directly perceive the Buddha
of Infinite Light.

O all you Buddhas and Bodhisattvas
of the ten directions, please grant your blessings
so that the wishes which I have just expressed
may be accomplished without any obstacles.

Tayatha Pentsadriya Awa Bodhanayé Soha.

བསོད་ནམས་འདི་ཡིས་ཐམས་ཅད་གཟིགས་པ་ཉིད།

sönam diyi tamché zikpa nyi

ཐོབ་ནས་ཉེས་པའི་དགྲ་རྣམས་ཕམ་བྱས་ནས།

tobné nyépé dranam pam jé né

སྐྱེ་ག་ན་འཆིའི་རྦ་རླབས་འཁྲུགས་པ་ཡི།

kyé ga na chi'i balab trouk pa yi

སྲིད་པའི་མཚོ་ལས་འགྲོ་བ་སྒྲོལ་བར་ཤོག།

sipé tsolé drowa drölwar sho

བྱང་ཆུབ་སེམས་མཆོག་རིན་པོ་ཆེ།

jangchoub sem chok rinpoché

མ་སྐྱེས་པ་རྣམས་སྐྱེ་གྱུར་ཅིག།

ma kyé pa nam kyé gyour chik

སྐྱེས་པ་ཉམས་པ་མེད་པ་དང་།

kyépa nyampa mépa tang

གོང་ནས་གོང་དུ་འཕེལ་བར་ཤོག།

gong né gong dou pelwar sho

Dedication

Through this merit, may I attain true omniscience.
Then, having overcome all harmful, destructive forces,
may I liberate sentient beings from the ocean of existence
and its turbulent waves of birth, old age,
sickness and death.

May the most precious mind of awakening
that has not yet dawned now arise.
Once arisen, may it never decline;
may it continue to increase evermore.

The 15th Karmapa, Khakhyab Dorjé

Continual Rain
for the Benefit of Beings

A condensed manual on
**Extending Throughout Space
for the Benefit of Beings,**
the meditation-recitation of Noble, Supreme Chenrezig,
according to the direct transmission of Tangtong Gyalpo,
Powerful Lord of Accomplishments

Svasti!
I bow down before the Venerable Protector
who is inseparable from He of the Sacred Activity
which Overturns the Depths of Samsara:
Avalokita, Chenrezig, who has arisen as the
manifest expression of the consummate compassion
of all Buddhas, the Victorious Ones.

Amongst all Victorious Ones, it is he whose mind of awakening and enlightened activity are most excellent. Rather than engaging in the stable meditative state of tranquility, he continuously practices the enlightened activity of past, present, and future which guides the six categories of beings until samsara has been emptied.

As confirmed by the prophecy of Buddha Shakyamuni,[1] he has been invested with power in the realm of the Tibetans,[2] the homeland of those who are very difficult to discipline. Since taking control of it and making it his noble sphere of influence, he has concretely carried out his activity in manifold forms, such as king, minister, translator, scholar, accomplished practitioner, and male and female youth. The potency of his blessing is such that as soon as they are able to speak, young children may spontaneously exclaim the six-syllable king of mantras[3] without ever having learned it.

---

1 Literally: the Victorious Companion of the Sun.
2 Literally: the land of the red-faced ones.
3 Om Mani Padmé Hung

The Great Compassionate Lord alone is considered to be the preordained deity of these snowy lands. This is why the eminent incarnate ones of the past have clearly presented countless forms, lengthy and concise, of the Noble One's practice cycle.

Of these, the practice explained here is the meditation-recitation called "Extending Throughout Space for the Benefit of Beings," composed by Chenrezig himself who came to help people in the guise of Tangtong Gyalpo, Lord of Accomplishments.

The practice is comprised of six parts:
1. The opening: refuge and bodhicitta;
2. The main part: deity meditation and
3. mantra recitation;
4. The conclusion: implementing the practice as the path and
5. dedicating the roots of virtue;
6. and an explanation of the benefits.

The First Part:
Taking Refuge and Developing Bodhicitta,
the Mind of Awakening
In the sky in front of us, amidst clouds of rainbows and flowers, is Noble Chenrezig, Avalokiteshvara, inseparable from our root lama. He manifests as the very nature, the embodiment, of all Victorious Buddhas, the rare and sublime three jewels, and the three roots[1] of all times and directions. We ourselves are present as the principal figure, surrounded by our enemies, loved ones and all those in between; that is, a great gathering of all beings belonging to the six realms.

Lama Chenrezig is the one who has the strength and capacity to protect us from samsara, the great ocean of suffering. Therefore, with absolute commitment of body, speech and mind, we take refuge with these three qualities: 1) the faith of totally entrusting [ourselves to him] as our only salvation; 2) our aspiration, formulated as "please protect us"; and 3) the confidence that we will truly be protected.

We recite:

Until I have reached full awakening, I take refuge
in the Buddha, the Dharma, and the supreme Assembly.

---

1 The Three Jewels: Buddha, Dharma and Sangha. The Three Roots: Lama, Yidam and Dakini or Dharmapala, Dharma Protector.

as many times as is appropriate. With firm conviction, we think: henceforth, all sentient beings and I myself are under the protection of the Noble, Great Compassionate One.

We consider the beings that are visualized before us and reflect: Among all of these, there is not a single one who has not been my kind parent. Their only desire is to be happy and be rid of suffering, yet all they do is create the causes for more suffering. The result is the sharp agony of samsara and the unfortunate realms: torment with no means of escape.

We think: I will do whatever it takes to establish them in the greatest happiness of all: the state of perfect, supreme enlightenment. However, since I do not currently have the capacity to achieve this, I will practice the profound meditation-recitation of Noble Chenrezig and attain the genuine state of the Supreme Noble One. For as long as samsara exists, I will strive to bring about the welfare of beings by emulating the enlightened example of Chenrezig.

With this intense, uncontrived aspiration, in the presence of Lama Chenrezig we vow to develop bodhicitta, saying:

Through the merit resulting from this meditation-recitation, may I attain enlightenment in order to benefit beings.

We recite this a number of times, clearly bearing in mind the sense of the meditation.

Multiple light rays shine forth from Lama Chenrezig's body and touch all the beings we have visualized, so that their negativities, veils and pain are purified and they all become happy. We imagine that the field of refuge then melts into light and dissolves into us. In this way, our mindstream has been blessed.

The Second Part: Deity Meditation
As during refuge, we imagine ourselves in our ordinary form surrounded by beings of the six realms, the objects of our compassion. Above each being is an eight-petaled white lotus in full bloom, with anthers and stamens. At its center is an immaculate full moon disc,[2] and atop this is the letter HRI, as white as pearl and resplendent with light. We are aware that [the HRI] appears as the very embodiment of the power and might of all Victorious Ones gathered into one.

---

2 Shamar Rinpoché explains that in ancient iconography the 'moon disc' actually referred to the top of the lotus seed pod which was depicted as being white, shiny and flat like the surface of a mirror.

A countless number of light rays shine like moonbeams from this letter, making offerings to all of the mandalas of the Victorious Ones of the ten directions and delighting their body, speech and mind. The rays then touch us all, purifying every one of our physical and mental illnesses, negativities and veils. As they encompass every space of the six realms where there are sentient beings, they clear away all suffering and endow every being with happiness.

The blessing of the assembly of the Noble Ones gathers again as light. This then dissolves into the letter HRI which crowns the head of each being, instantaneously transforming it into the form of the Noble, Supreme Chenrezig, as superbly white as sun shining on snow and dazzling with light. His body emanates light rays of the five colors that fill the pure fields of the Buddhas and inspire the Noble Ones to accomplish the welfare of beings. Light also fills the six realms of beings below, clearing away all suffering and establishing happiness throughout.

He is delightedly smiling at me and all beings. With lovingkindness towards us all like a mother's love for her only child, he constantly takes in the whole of the three times with all-seeing eyes.

The first two of his four arms are held, palms together, at the level of his heart. His lower right hand holds a crystal rosary; his lower left hand holds an eight-petaled white lotus with its stem. He is adorned with silken ribbons and an upper garment of white silk embroidered with gold; his lower robes are of red silk.

Every part of his body is fully graced with the various ornaments made of gold from the Dzambu river:[1] a crown studded with assorted celestial gems; earrings; short, medium and long necklaces; arm bands, bracelets and anklets; and a belt with garlands of small bells that tinkle melodiously. The golden-hued skin of the krishnasara deer[2] covers the left side of his chest. Part of his hair is bound in a knot; the rest falls freely.

---

1 That is, the purest and finest of all kinds of gold. Of a slightly reddish hue, it is found in a legendary river.
2 The krishnasara is a mythical deer or antelope said to be the most compassionate of animals. The krishnasara purportedly takes great pains to avoid harming any other being, and always steps carefully to avoid crushing insects or other small creatures.

Crowning his head is the Buddha Amitabha, lord of the family,[3] in the attire of supreme nirmanakaya.[4] Chenrezig is seated with his legs crossed in the adamantine posture.[5] A backrest consisting of an immaculate, perfectly full moon disc supports his body.[6]

Thinking that he personifies the very essence of the Buddha, the Dharma and the Sangha brought together, the sources of refuge of the three times and ten directions, we recite:

Upon a white lotus and moon above my head
and crowning each sentient being throughout space,
is HRI from which Noble, Supreme Chenrezig appears,
gleaming white and radiating five-colored light.
Lovely and smiling, he gazes with eyes of compassion.
The first two of his four hands are held palms together,
the lower two hold a crystal rosary and white lotus.
Adorned with silk and jewel ornaments,
his upper body is clothed with a deerskin.
His head is crowned with Buddha Amitabha,
and he is seated in the adamantine posture
with an immaculate full moon as his backrest.
In essence he is the union of all sources of refuge.

Taking our time, we read and visualize distinctly each aspect of his physical form.

The Third Part: Mantra Recitation

There are two sections of mantra recitation: invoking the mindstream of the deity through prayer, and practicing the deity yoga of the three doors through sending out and gathering back.

As for the first, all beings and I myself address Noble and Supreme Chenrezig, the lama who has been envisioned as above. In unison, with perfectly focused minds, we think: You know what is to be done. Our welfare is entirely in your

---

3 Each of the five Buddha families—buddha, ratna, padma, karma and vajra—is presided over by one of the five Wisdom Buddhas. Amitabha is lord of the padma, or lotus, family to which Chenrezig belongs.
4 That is, clothed in monk's robes and holding an alms bowl.
5 The adamantine, or vajrasana, posture is akin to the full lotus: left foot on right thigh and right foot folded over the left leg, resting on the left thigh.
6 According to Shamar Rinpoché, this backrest refers in fact to the golden chair of the highest members of Indian royalty who were called chakravartin, or universal emperors.

hands. Please deliver us from the six samsaric realms and guide us to the enlightened state of complete omniscience.

As many times as we can—a hundred, twenty-one, seven, etc.—until our mind becomes compliant and our perception is truly transformed, we recite:

Lord of pure white, undefiled and flawless,
your head is crowned with the perfect Buddha.
You gaze upon beings with eyes of compassion:
Chenrezig, I bow down before you.

If we have the possibility and the wish, we may add Gélong-ma Palmo's Potö Hymn, Lopön Dawa's Lamentation, or other sacred hymns. It seems to me that any of these very inspiring prayers that hold great blessing are welcome additions.

The second part is accomplishing the deity yoga of the three doors[1] through the practice of sending out and gathering back [light rays]. After having one-pointedly prayed to and invoked him as described, innumerable light rays of the five colors, predominantly white, emanate from the body of the Noble One above our heads. The instant they touch all beings and myself, it is like the light of a torch illuminating the darkness.

Everything that is impure, all negativities and veils due to wrongful actions, all faults and transgressions born of disturbing emotions, all of this, whatever it may be, is purified in one instant.

This includes all negative actions perpetrated by myself and others since beginningless time: the five most negative acts of direct consequence[2] and those belonging to the ten non-virtuous acts. These are the three of the body: killing, taking what has not been given, and sexual misconduct; the four of speech: telling outlandish lies that injure lamas and other people, sowing dissension amongst familiars through slander, saying unkind things that hurt others' feelings, and spouting nonsense; and the three of the mind: envy, where one covets other people's wealth and belongings; malice, where one thinks up ways to harm others; and wrong views consisting of

---

1 Body, speech, and mind.
2 Traditionally considered the five most heinous acts are: killing one's mother, killing one's father, killing an arhat (one whose realization is such that they are liberated from cyclic existence), drawing a Buddha's blood through aggression, and creating a schism in a community of the Buddha's disciples. They are called 'boundless acts of direct consequence' because perpetrators are said to go directly to the hell realm after death, without passing through an intermediate state.

disbelieving or negating the advantages of liberation and the disadvantages of wrongdoing.

Obscurations result from improper conduct based on desire-attachment, anger-aversion, ignorance, pride or jealousy. These include acts which are formally prohibited and those which are not, but are considered transgressions because they are inherently unwholesome. They eclipse the well-being of the upper realms and the path to liberation.

Downfalls entail disrespect for vows which have been taken: vows of individual liberation, bodhisattva vows, and vows of vajrayana; or neglecting these through carelessness. As a result of not observing them, one will fall into the lower realms.

Offenses consist of going against the minor precepts. Although they do not result in falling into the lower states, they delay the attainment of enlightenment.

The confused karmic tendency of dualism, together with the obscuration of incomplete knowing, has fostered clinging to self and other as subject and object since beginningless time. This is purified, and the blessing that creatively manifests as inseparability from the body, speech and mind of Lord Chenrezig is granted. We clearly become the physical form of the Noble One, the rainbow-like union of appearance and emptiness, extending throughout all places where beings of the six realms, as numerous as the sky is vast, reside. Our environment—the outer vessel of the myriad worlds—becomes none other than the highest realm, the Land of Joy, Dewachen. It is of the nature of precious gems and rainbow-colored light; the very notion of earth, mountains, and rocks is unheard of here.

All sentient beings of the six realms—that is, all inhabitants[3] [of the myriad world systems]—are liberated from their specific forms of suffering and their bodies instantly become the body of the Noble One of Great Compassion. All sounds, whether the speech of beings or the sounds of the phenomenal world, are expressed as the very resonance of the six-syllable secret mantra. As the concept-dependent, confused aspect of mind is purified, our insight manifests as the mind of the Noble One, the inseparable union of awareness and emptiness.

---

3 The term used here for "environments and inhabitants" is literally "vessels and contents."

Thus, the body, speech and mind of others and oneself are none other than the pure aspect of manifestation appearing as the body and pure realm of the deity; the pure aspect of sound as the secret mantra; and the pure aspect of mind as naked awareness-emptiness.

As we settle into the inconceivable, all-encompassing great expanse free of grasping, we recite:

As the result of this perfectly focused invocation,
light radiates from the body of the Noble One
clearing away impure karmic experience and misconceptions.

The outer universe manifests as Dewachen, the Realm of Joy,
and the body, speech and mind of the beings who live there
are the enlightened body, speech and mind of Lord Chenrezig.
Appearance, sound and awareness are inseparable
from emptiness.

Having clearly visualized the points explained above, we recite the mantra **Om Mani Padmé Hung** as the main part of the practice session.

Concerning this six-letter secret mantra, it is Noble Chenrezig who uniquely embodies the powers of timeless wisdom of all Buddhas. The potent strength of his compassion and all forms of his enlightened activity are concentrated in and expressed by the six-syllable secret mantra.

OM is white. The letter that unites enlightened qualities, it arises from the natural dynamism of the Noble One's five wisdoms. It is the nature of the paramita[1] of meditative stability. It purifies the emotion of pride as cause, as well as its general karmic results. More specifically, it purifies the suffering of the gods: the transition and fall from the god realms.

It is none other than the form and enlightened activity of Indra, Ruler of a Hundred Sacrifices, Sage of the Gods. It manifests as the image of the Wisdom of Equality's inherent radiance. It guides the six families of beings to the Glorious Buddhafield of the south, and leads them to attain the form of Buddha Ratnasambhava.

---

1 The paramitas are the transcendent qualities to be perfected on the path to awakening. Traditionally, in Bodhisattvayana Buddhism there are generally six qualities; certain sutras speak of ten. Each syllable of Chenrezig's mantra embodies the essence of one of the six paramitas.

MA is green. The letter of enlightened activity, it arises from the Noble One's compassion as the expression of his immeasurable love for all beings. It is the nature of the paramita of patience. It purifies the emotion of jealousy as cause, as well as its general karmic results. More specifically, it purifies the suffering of the demigods: quarrels and conflict.

It is none other than the form and enlightened activity of Vemacitra, Splendid Robe, Sage of the Demigods. It manifests as the image of All-Accomplishing Wisdom's inherent radiance. It guides the six families of beings to the Buddhafield of Consummate Activity in the north, and leads them to attain the form of Buddha Amoghasiddhi.

NI is yellow. It arises from the natural dynamism of the Noble One's great compassion, all-embracing and effortless. It is adamantine wisdom, the union of enlightened body, speech, mind, qualities and activity. It is the letter that automatically transmutes samsara into nirvana, the sphere beyond suffering. It is the nature of the paramita of moral discipline. It purifies the taint of ignorance—dualistic clinging—as cause, as well as its general karmic results. More specifically, it purifies the four great rivers of human suffering that are birth, aging, sickness and death. It is none other than the form and enlightened activity of Buddha Shakyamuni, Sage of the Humans.

It manifests as the image of the inherent radiance of Naturally Present Wisdom. It guides the six families of beings to Akanishtha, the Unsurpassable, the perfectly pure Buddhafield of Dharmadhatu, and leads them to attain the form of Vajradhara, the sixth Buddha.

PAD is clear blue. The letter of enlightened body, it arises from the natural dynamism of immeasurable equanimity: the Noble One's perfectly impartial compassion. It is the nature of the paramita of superior knowledge. It purifies the emotion of ignorance as cause, as well as its general karmic results. More specifically, it purifies the suffering associated with the animal realm: dullness, speechlessness and servitude.

It is none other than the form and enlightened activity of Shravasinha, Steadfast Lion, Sage of the Animals. It manifests as the image of the Wisdom of Dharmadhatu's inherent radiance. It guides the six families of beings to the Densely Arrayed Buddhafield in the center, and leads them to attain the form of Buddha Vairocana.

MÉ is red. The letter of enlightened speech, it arises from the natural dynamism of immeasurable joy, the Noble One's uniform compassion towards all. It is the nature of the paramita of generosity. It purifies desire-attachment, greed and stinginess as cause, as well as their general karmic results. More specifically, it purifies the suffering of the hungry spirits: hunger and thirst.

It is none other than the form and enlightened activity of Jvalamukhadeva, Blazing Mouth, Sage of the Hungry Spirits. It manifests as the image of Discriminating Wisdom's inherent radiance. It guides the six families of beings to Dewachen, the Realm of Joy in the west, and leads them to attain the form of Buddha Amitabha.

HUNG is black. The letter of enlightened mind, it arises from the natural dynamism of the Noble One's compassion, the immeasurable compassion that watches over all beings as one's own child. It is the nature of the paramita of superior knowledge. It purifies dualistic anger-aversion as cause, as well as its general karmic results. More specifically, it purifies the suffering endured by those in the hell realms: extreme heat and cold.

It is none other than the form and enlightened activity of Dharmaraja, King of Dharma, Sage of the Hell Realms. It manifests as the image of Mirror-Like Wisdom's inherent radiance. It guides the six families of beings to the Buddha-field of True Joy, Abhirati, and leads them to attain the form of Buddha Akshobhya.

In this way, the six-syllable mantra, king of all secret mantras, is the quintessence of the force and might of the immeasurable enlightened activity that extricates the beings of the six families from the very depths of samsara. Therefore, it should be recited as much as possible during the main part of a practice session.

At the end, light emanating from the body of Lama Chenrezig above our heads dissolves the whole phenomenal universe, visualized as enlightened physical forms and pure realms, into light. This melts into Lama Chenrezig who dissolves into light. This light melts into us, then we ourselves dissolve into light. It is the clear light of emptiness itself, free of the three spheres of focus[1] that grasp self and other, deity and mantra.

---

1 Subject, object and action.

It is devoid of all fabricated, characteristic-based reference points, such as existent/nonexistent, being/not being, empty/not empty. It is the indivisibility of appearance, sound, awareness and emptiness, free of observer and observed. We remain in this experience of absorption for as long as we can within the natural essence of great, all-encompassing dharmadhatu, the very mind of the Noble One.

The Fourth Part: Conclusion, Making Practice the Path

When we emerge from this state, we maintain the meditative experience wherein every material thing composed of the five elements that appears to oneself and others—such as earth, rocks, mountains, boulders, and so on—is united in the physical form of the Noble, Great Compassionate One. All sounds, those made by living beings and those arising from inanimate phenomena, are the melody of the Six Syllable Mantra: the speech of the Noble One. All thoughts and concepts are unconditioned awareness-emptiness, the fundamental nature of dharmakaya: the mind of the Noble One.

When traveling, walking, sleeping, sitting, talking or communicating—that is, while engaging in any kind of activity—we abandon ordinary conceptual clinging and embrace the deep concentration of three-fold awareness,[2] as expressed by:

Our physical forms are the body of the Noble One,
all sounds are the melody of the six syllables,
and thoughts are the vast expanse of great wisdom.

The Fifth Part: Dedicating the Roots of Virtue to Enlightenment and Making Wishing Prayers

All of the goodness accumulated in our mindstream by having practiced this meditation-recitation is dedicated equally to all beings. Through this unsurpassable accumulation of merit, may we rapidly attain the paramount state equal to that of Lord Chenrezig. May we acquire the power and ability to establish all beings, without a single exception, in numbers as great as the sky is vast, in the state synonymous with that of Great Compassion, the Noble Supreme One: in genuine, perfect enlightenment.

---

2 Appearance, sound and thought as the body/environment, speech and mind of the deity.

Thinking this, we recite:

*Through this virtue, may I swiftly attain the state
of Lord Chenrezig,
and may I establish all beings, without a single exception,
in this state.*

We conclude by adding as many pure wishing prayers as possible.

Those who cannot practice as just described should begin by taking refuge and developing bodhicitta as explained above. For the main part of the practice, imagine that Noble, Supreme Chenrezig, as described in the texts, is settled above your head. With a mind perfectly concentrated on the corresponding supplication, make a few aspiration prayers while thinking: Lama Chenrezig, please heed me!

Alternatively, OM is understood to be the letter that unifies the wisdoms of the five kayas; MANI means jewel; and PADMÉ means having or holding a lotus. Holder of the Jewel and the Lotus is Noble Chenrezig's name. HUNG is the mantra of activity which protects beings from the suffering of the six realms.

Recite as many six-syllable mantras as possible while bearing the meaning of this supplication in mind: O Holder of the Jewel and the Lotus, personification of the five kayas and five wisdoms, please give beings of the six families refuge from suffering!

In the end, Lama Chenrezig above your head is overjoyed. He dissolves into light and this melts into you. With this, imagine sincerely that the wisdom of the Noble One has entered your mindstream—have no doubt! Follow with the dedication and wishing prayers.

Because it is certain that you will obtain the benefits described below, please do this practice with reverence and joy!

The Sixth Part: Explanation of the Benefits
The full benefit of practicing the meditation-recitation of Noble Chenrezig as described is inestimable. The substance of the benefit of contemplating the body of the deity and doing his meditation is expressed in a few words in the Lotus Lattice root tantra:

> All Buddhas are included in the practice
> of just one mandala of enlightened body:
> that of the body of Chenrezig, the Protector.

By doing his practice and bearing him in mind,
even the most negative acts of direct consequence
are purified.

The benefit of reciting the six syllables, king of all secret mantras, was explained by the Victorious One, the flawless voice of the perfect Buddha Shakyamuni: the illustrious master Guru Rinpoché, Mahaguru Padmasambhava, in the form of a testament to the people of Tibet. His treasure teaching, revealed by the undisputed great revealer of treasures who manifested as Vidyadhara Jatsön Nyingpo, states:

OM MANI PADMÉ HUNG.

This six-syllable mantra is the unique quintessence of the wisdom mind of all Buddhas. It is the unique quintessence of the eighty-four thousand root teachings of the Dharma. It is the very heart of the Buddhas of the five families and the Lords of Secrets.

Essential pith instructions are concentrated in each of the six syllables. The mantra is the source of all good fortune and qualities. It is the root of accomplishment of all benefit and happiness. It is the great path to the fortunate realms and to liberation.

Through hearing even once the supreme expression of the six syllables, essence of all of the teachings of the Dharma, one attains the level of no return[1] and becomes a guide who leads beings to liberation.

Any animal, even an ant, who hears it when dying will be reborn in Dewachen once it has passed on.

Simply recalling the six-syllable mantra is like the sun shining on snow; all of the negative deeds and obscurations born of the accumulation of negative actions perpetrated during all existences within samsara since beginningless time are purified and one is reborn in Dewachen, the Realm of Joy.

Moreover, touching it is like receiving empowerments from countless Buddhas and Bodhisattvas. Contemplating it only once is like hearing, reflecting and meditating: everything which appears arises as Dharmakaya.

It is an open treasure-hold of enlightened activity that benefits beings.

---

1 An extremely stable level of realization from which regression is impossible.

Also, from the same source:

> Child of noble family, it would be possible to calculate the weight of Mount Meru, the King of Mountains, on a scale, but it is impossible to measure the merit resulting from a single recitation of the six-syllable mantra.
>
> It would be possible to wear away a diamond boulder by sliding a soft cloth of Benares muslin over it once every hundred years,
> but it is impossible to measure the merit resulting from a single recitation of the six-syllable mantra.
>
> It would be possible to take all the water out of a great ocean drop by drop,
> but it is impossible to deplete the merit resulting from a single recitation of the six-syllable mantra.
>
> It would be possible to count every particle contained in the snowy lands of the Himalayas, and every leaf of their thickets and forests,
> but it is impossible to measure the amount of merit resulting from a single recitation of the six-syllable mantra.
>
> Likewise, it would be possible to empty a storehouse a hundred leagues long that is filled with sesame by discarding one seed a day,
> but it is impossible to measure the amount of merit resulting from a single recitation of the six-syllable mantra.
>
> It would be possible to count every raindrop that falls during twelve months of rain,
> but it is impossible to measure the amount of merit resulting from a single recitation of the six-syllable mantra.
>
> Thus it is, child of noble family! There is no need to discuss it night and day!
>
> Still, it would be possible to calculate the merit resulting from the practice of someone like me who may have worshipped and served ten million Tathagathas . . .
> but it is impossible to measure the amount of merit resulting from a single recitation of the six-syllable mantra.
>
> Through it, the doors to rebirth in the six realms are blocked,
> the paths and bhumis[1] of the six paramitas are traversed,

---

1 The paths and bhumis (literally "grounds") are distinct spiritual levels traversed as bodhisattvas progress toward complete awakening.

the defilements of habitual tendencies of karma and
afflictions are purified,
and the pure realms of the three kayas are accomplished.

Children of noble family: listen well!

Thanks to the blessing of all Victorious Ones,
this heart of the innermost quintessence
is the source of all happiness and benefit.
It is the root of all spiritual accomplishments,
the ladder leading to the superior realms,
the gate that blocks access to the unfortunate realms,
the ship that delivers from samsara,
the lamp that clears away the darkness,
the hero that triumphs over the five poisons,
the bonfire that burns away negativities and veils,
the sledgehammer that strikes down suffering,
the remedy that tempers the uncivilized.

It is the destined Dharma of the Snowy Lands.
It is the quintessential heart nectar
of all of the many sutras, tantras, and treatises,
and of listening, reflecting and practicing.
It is the precious monarch that suffices unto itself.
Please recite these six syllables!

. . . and so on.

The abundant references found in the canons and treasure
teachings cannot all be expressed. If the enlightened speech
that is this six-syllable mantra is recited just once with
true faith, the benefits described herein will most certainly
emerge. By not leaving our body, speech and mind in the ordinary state, a minimum of effort will result in an immense,
deeply meaningful accumulation of merit. I would ask you
to do whatever you can to give your human existence true
meaning and take the pledge to practice from one hundred to
ten thousand mantras each and every day!

May the lifeline of Noble Chenrezig's compassion
draw all beings from the ocean of existence.
May it lead them to shelter on Potala Mountain,
the perfectly free land of joyful deliverance.

The Dharma practitioner of noble family, Kalzang Drölkar,
together with her mother, Tséten Drölkar-la, entreated me
to compose something of this sort. After a great deal of time
and many earnestly repeated requests, this was composed in
my spare time so that a simple layman like myself could

easily understand it. It comes from the paw of the sickly old fellow, the beggar disguised as a practitioner called Lodrö Ziji, alias Khakhyab Dorjé, who pretends to be a bodhisattva in these declining times.

May goodness and excellence increase!

Printed in the USA
CPSIA information can be obtained
at www.ICGtesting.com
LVHW071930261023
762086LV00009B/23